David Benda Malonga

Design and production of a prize list management application

David Benda Malonga

Design and production of a prize list management application

The town of LIKASI

ScienciaScripts

Imprint

Any brand names and product names mentioned in this book are subject to trademark, brand or patent protection and are trademarks or registered trademarks of their respective holders. The use of brand names, product names, common names, trade names, product descriptions etc. even without a particular marking in this work is in no way to be construed to mean that such names may be regarded as unrestricted in respect of trademark and brand protection legislation and could thus be used by anyone.

Cover image: www.ingimage.com

This book is a translation from the original published under ISBN 978-620-6-70724-0.

Publisher:
Sciencia Scripts
is a trademark of
Dodo Books Indian Ocean Ltd. and OmniScriptum S.R.L publishing group

120 High Road, East Finchley, London, N2 9ED, United Kingdom
Str. Armeneasca 28/1, office 1, Chisinau MD-2012, Republic of Moldova, Europe
Printed at: see last page
ISBN: 978-620-7-79610-6

EPIGRAPH

"Science without conscience is but the ruin of the soul".

[Francois Rabelais]

Alicia NKULU VUELE

DEDICATION

To the NKULU VUELE family

Alicia NKULU VUELE

FOREWORD

As is customary in the Democratic Republic of the Congo, a student wishing to obtain a diploma in any field of study, and in our case especially ibusiness informatics, is required to produce a scientific paper assessing the knowledge and skills acquired during his or her years of learning at university. It is with this in mind that we have written this paper.

Humans invented writing as a means of preserving the great authors and their experiences of life's phenomena. In this way, the world's information and know-how is written down in sideboards and cupboards.

Nowadays, the world is becoming more and more like a small village, thanks to the privileges of information technology. In view of the world's current technological evolution, computing has become an indispensable element in the evolution of the universe, which man has always sought to improve through the invention of various machines since ancient times. Today, man has succeeded beyond conception in creating a machine that can automatically and rationally process information using programs stored in its precious tool, the computer. At present, all companies are interested in this tool, to make their management more flexible, and it is with this same means of information processing that we are going to create an application for managing agents' services.

ACKNOWLEDGEMENTS

We thank the Eternal God, Almighty, for his grace which he has granted us until the end of our work.

Our thanks also go to the rector of the Université Chrétienne source de Vie, Dr MULOPWE DIBWE, to the academic general secretary, Dr Eric MPYANA, and to the entire faculty of the university.

We would like to thank the Université Chrétienne source de Vie for the training courses organized.

We would like to thank our director Mr. Theodore MWANZA KALEJA for his assistance, guidance and advice, without which this work would not have seen the light of day.

We'd like to thank you, our dearest parents Mr Guillaume NKULU VUELE and Mrs Gorety MONGA MPANGA, for your affection, love and everything you've done for us.

Our thanks also go to my brothers and sisters: Irène MONGA and her husband Pierre LUBABA, Guillaumetine NGOY, Nathalie MONGA and her husband Pascale NSWANA, Djo NUMBI, Chadrack NKULU, Otiniel UMBA, Cledia ILUNGA and our youngest daughter Abigael MPANGA.

Our thanks go straight to you, Mr Venas NYEMBO ALIMASI, for your material, financial and moral support.

We would like to express our sincere thanks to all our dear colleagues. We can't name all the people who have helped and encouraged us in one way or another, but we'd like to thank them all.

ACRONYMS

UP: Unified Process

UML: Unified Modeling Language

TFC: Travail de Fin de Cycle

HTML : Hyper Text Markup Language

WWW: World Wide Web

CSS: Cascading Style Sheets

HTML : Hypertext Markup Language

DBMS: Database Management System

DML: Data Manipulation Language

LDD: Data Description Language

IBM: International Business Machine

RDBMS: Relational Database Management System

SQL : Structured Query Language

MySQL : Microsoft Structured Query Language

MVC: Model View Controller

DAL: Data Access Layer

UI: User Interface

BLL: Business Logic Layer

TCP: Transfer Control Protocol

IP: Internet Protocol

HTTP: HyperText Transfer Protocol

PHP : HyperText Preprocessor

TABLE OF CONTENTS

GENERAL INTRODUCTION

1. GENERAL

Nowadays, the world is experiencing considerable technological progress in all sectors, thanks to computer science, which studies automatic information processing techniques. It plays an important role in the development of businesses and other institutions.

Before the invention of the computer, all information was recorded manually on paper, which caused many problems, such as wasting a lot of time searching for information, damaging the information, etc.

Over the last thirty years, business computing has undergone considerable upheaval. Technological advances in information processing have had a major impact on the role of IT in the world. While the first applications were used to automate the operational activities of organizations (production management, sales and financial management, customer management, human resources, etc.), today's information systems take on increasingly strategic levels of management. The development of information technology has led to the creation of new hardware and software that minimize information processing time, an essential step in modern project management.

So, to this day, the computer remains the most reliable means of processing and storing information. This invention has made it possible to computerize corporate data systems, which is an essential part of their development today.

In the educational context, IT makes available digital tools and products that can be used to improve the quality of education.

IT has thus become the means par excellence for optimizing information processing within organizations. These organizations have seen their sales increase as a result. Equipping oneself with IT tools has, so to speak, become a race towards evolution.

The sub-division, also being an organization, is no exception to the rule. So, with a view to alleviating the problems it encounters in its management, our subject is entitled: "*the design and implementation of an application to monitor pupils' schooling*", with Likasi I sub-division as the case study.

2. STATUS OF THE QUESTION

The state of the question is an examination of the question and a review of previous literature on the subject in question, in order to identify the originality of the author's work in relation to others. This effort spares the author the need to revisit trades already covered; in short, unnecessary repetition from a scientific point of view."[1] .

In this part of our work, we draw a line with previous work.

➢ NDAYA ILUNGA IRÈNE spoke on "the design and implementation of a prize list production application", a case study from the NDOTO institute.

- This work has as problematic:

▪ The management and tracking of data concerning the institute is difficult due to poor data storage technology; information is recorded on paper.

▪ Producing and transmitting the various reports between players takes far too much time.

▪ The loss of certain documents after a lapse of time, due to the nature of the medium. In fact, in an old school like NDOTO, the management of activities in the area of prize list productivity is still manual, which makes the work repetitive and tedious, given the importance of the subject and the number of students.

The hypothesis of this work was to set up a system to solve the problems associated with producing the prize list.

The aforementioned researcher addressed the subject of ranking management in the same way as above, but for our purposes, we'll emphasize that we're not just interested in the ranking management of a single school, but in the ranking management of several schools (the scope of this subject being on schools scattered over an entire city).

3. CHOICE AND INTEREST OF SUBJECT
3.1 Choice of subject

The choice of this subject was born of personal motivation after participant observation within the functional system of the Likasi I sub-division, as well as the declining educational level of pupils in the Democratic Republic of Congo in general, and in the town of Likasi in particular.

---

[1] KAZADI KIMBU and KALUNGA MAWAZO, *research and analysis methods in the social and human sciences. humaines : une lecture de la critologie de la scientificité intersubjective,*EDUPC /lubumbashi,2013 ,p.117

3.2 The subject's interests

a. Self-interest

This work enabled us to reconcile the theories we had learned with the practical aspects of our three years of study. What's more, on completion of the project, we will be awarded the title of Graduate in Business Informatics.

b. Scientific interest

From a scientific point of view, this work is a reference for future researchers.

c. Social interests

The results of this study will enable sub-division managers to improve their management through the application to be developed, and schools to consult the catalog without having to travel.

4. ISSUES AND HYPOTHESIS

a. Issues

The problematic is a set of questions and issues that the researcher asks himself about his object of study. It can be formulated in a single question or in several[2] . It is a set of preoccupations and concerns that the researcher addresses throughout his work, with a view to resolving them.

During our field trip we identified the following problems
following ;

➤ Considerable time wasted searching for information:
Every year, there's a real need to record information. A school has many pupils, and all these pupils need to be memorized to better track their progress. Since management is manual, it's hard to find information about a pupil from a particular year or school.

Given the multiplicity of schools and pupils, and the manual management of information processing currently practiced within the sub-division, finding an item in record time is not only difficult, but also hypothetical.

---

[2] KAZADI KIMBU and KALUNGA MAWAZO, *Les méthodes de recherche et d'analyse en sciences sociales et humaines*, EDUPC/Lubumbashi, 2013, p.108

➢ Difficulty in registering schools and pupils

Each school must be known. The sub-division is supposed to hold all the information on pupils from the various schools scattered across the city. At present, however, it is impossible to have an overview of all this information.

Thus, our research will revolve around the following research question: what tool can we provide to the registration of primary, secondary and technical education, Likasi I sub-division, in order to ensure efficient and effective monitoring of pupils' schooling?

b. Hypothesis

The research hypothesis is defined as "the proposed answers to the question we ask about the object of the research, formulated in such terms that observation and analysis can provide an answer".[3]

In view of the above-mentioned problems, computerization of the department responsible for managing the school curriculum of pupils enrolled in primary, secondary and technical education in the urban city of Likasi would be the expected solution, and would significantly reduce the number of cases of fraud linked to the management of pupils' files.

In concrete terms, the aim is to set up a web application tmanage the publication of students' results, with a view to significantly reducing the number of cases where classes are overlapped in the various schools within its jurisdiction.

5. RESEARCH METHODS AND TECHNIQUES

5.1 METHODS

In terms of philosophical representation, method comprises the set of intellectual operations that a discipline implements to demonstrate, verify and establish the truths it pursues. From this conception, method appears as a set of rules independent of any research, but aimed at forms of reasoning that would make the reality to be grasped accessible[4] .

To achieve the objectives of our work, we used the UP (Unified Process) method, an information systems design method based on the UML language.

---

[3] RONGERE and MULUMBATI NG, *manuel sociologie général*, Ed. Africa, Lubumbashi 1980, P. 21.

[4] Ibrahima Lo, *Les méthodes de recherche scientifique en sciences sociales,* ed. Alto Aubier, Paris, 1995, p.17

5.2 TECHNIQUES

Methods should not be confused with techniques, which, as Robert PINTO and Madeleine GRAWITZ note, "are merely tools made available for research and organized by the method for this purpose"[5] .

1.   Interview technique

It refers to an interview in which the respondent orally provides information to the interviewer. It enabled us to gather information by interviewing sub-division staff. To gather information about our work, we interviewed the head of personnel, the head of SERNIE in the sub-division, and the director of studies at Nyele School.

2.   Observation technique

 This technique enabled us to observe processes as they unfolded, and to pinpoint problems with a view to remedying them.

3.   Documentary technique

This technique enabled us to complete our interview and observation by consulting certain documents and websites to further enrich our work.

6.   DELIMITATION

In order to meet the requirements of scientific rigor, we felt it necessary to subject our work to a special and temporal delimitation. As is recommended for all scientific work, the subject to be dealt with must be delimited both in special and temporal terms.

In terms of time, our study covers the period from December 2019 to October 2020, and looks at the information handled by the institute from 2018 to the present day.

From a spatial point of view, the present work is limited to the sub-division, particularly in the SERNIE service.

7.   LABOR SUBDIVISION

Apart from the introduction and general conclusion, the present work will revolve around four chapters:

---

[5] Jean-Louis Loubet del Bayle, Initiation aux méthodes des sciences sociales(2000), Toulouse

❖ Chapter 1: "Definition of concepts and theoretical considerations". This chapter is devoted to defining the main concepts used in the subject, as well as outlining the various theories discussed.

❖ Chapter 2: "Study of the existing system". This chapter presents the current curriculum management system within the sub-division.

❖ Third chapter: "Detailed design of the computer system" to ensure that the design and modelling approaches are properly implemented;

❖ Fourth chapter: "Implementing the computer system". In this chapter, we develop the application to achieve our goal.

CHAPTER ONE
CONCEPT DEFINITIONS AND THEORETICAL CONSIDERATIONS

I.1. INTRODUCTION

In this chapter, we first define the concepts so that our readers have a clear view of the content.

Secondly, we present the theories relevant to our subject.
In particular, those relating to the method used, the modeling language, etc.

I.2. DEFINITION OF BASIC CONCEPTS

➢ **Conception:** in social and human science, conception is the way of perceiving an idea; in biology and medicine, conception is synonymous with fertilization, i.e. the action by which a living being, a child, is conceived. In applied science and discipline, i.e. computer science, design is the process of creating drawings or projects, more specifically in the context of tangible or intangible products[6] .

➢ **Realization: the** act of moving something from the abstract to the concrete.

➢ **Application:** a program or set of programs designed to help a computer user perform a specific task[7] .

➢ **Follow-up**: is a set of operations consisting in monitoring and controlling a process to achieve the desired result in the best possible conditions.

➢ **A student's school curriculum:** a set of academic studies in a given field, often leading to a state diploma in the DRC.[8]

I.3 THEORETICAL CONSIDERATIONS

A. Information theories

It is a theory aiming at quantifying and qualifying the notion of information content present in a set of data without precision, is the usual name designating Shannon's information theory, which is a probabilistic theory allowing to quantify the average information content of a set of messages, whose computer coding satisfies a precise statistical distribution[9] .

---

[6] http:// Fr.m.Wikipedia.org/wiki/conception consulted on 03/02/2020 at 12 : 30.
[7] Http: www.larousse.fr/dictionnaire/français/application/176,consulté on 03/02/2020,15:00.
[8] https://cordial.fr/dictionnaire/definition/cursus.php consulted on 03/02/2020 at 18h00
[9] http://fr.wikipedia.org/wiki/theorie-de-27informatique consulted on 03/02/2020 at 19:50

B. Information system theory

A company is a complex system in which a great deal of information flows. Without a system to control these flows, the company can quickly become overwhelmed, and no longer operate with a satisfactory quality of service. The challenge for any company, whether trading, industrial or service, is to set up a system designed to collect, store, process and distribute information (with a sufficiently short response time). This information system provides the link between two other company systems: the operating system and the control system.

The information system is the set of human, technical and financial resources that supply, use, compile, process and distribute the organization's information. It feeds the organization with information from various sources (internal or external). It is the mandatory gateway for all corporate information[10] .

The information system must describe (or represent) the functioning of the operating system as accurately as possible. To do this, it must incorporate an information base in which to store the description of the objects, rules and constraints of the operating system. As this base is subject to change, the information system must be equipped with a mechanism (called an information processor) designed to manage and control these changes[11] .

C. Systems theory

In anatomy, a system designates a set of similar parts involved in common activity (cardiac system, digestive system, respiratory system, etc.). In science, the system can be used to define units, such as the metric system[12] .

A system is a finite element whose perimeter is a boundary separating it from its environment.

It interacts with its environment through incoming information flows, which it processes and returns to the environment in the form of outgoing information flows.

The system will generate information about its behavior, both within the environment and on its own behalf. A system communicates.

To make decisions, a system needs to store and process information.

---

[10] J.Batiste , *Merise, Guide pratique : modélisation des données et des traitements,* new edition, ENI, paris, P.6
[11] F.DIGALLO, Methodologie des systemes d'informations-merise,CNAM ANGOULEME, 2001-2002, Paris, P.7
[12] J.Batiste , *Merise, Guide pratique : modélisation des données et des traitements,* new edition, ENI, paris, P.6

Systems theory is defined as a theory as opposed to other theories, because it seeks rules of general value that can be applied to all types of systems and with any degree of reality. It should be noted that systems are composed of ordered modules of interdependent and interacting parts[13] .

D. UML NOTATION

In IT, UML (Unified Modeling Language) is a language for the upstream phases of software development. UML is a unified modeling technique derived from older methods such as OMT, OOSE and Booch. It is primarily a notation language for software engineering, but it is sufficiently complete to allow modeling of information systems in particular. The language was developed by Rational Software, the company that financed the merger of the software gurus of the end of the century: OOD(Booch), OMT(Rumbaugh) and OOSE2 (Jacobson). But the very open approach, thanks to the Internet, enabled many specialists to get involved. This modeling technique took the best from each of the methods that were waging a merciless war against each other.

In this notation, 9 diagram types are proposed to the designer for building a model with the Agile approach, only half of which are used, with particular emphasis on class and interaction diagrams. This deliberate limitation significantly reduces the time needed t o learn modeling with UML, while remaining more than sufficient for most projects. According to Pascal Roques, UML (Unified Modeling Language) is a graphical and textual modeling language for understanding and describing requirements, specifying and documenting systems, sketching software architectures, designing solutions and communicating points of view[14] .

A. Usefulness of UML[15]

UML is used to specify, visualize, modify and build the documents needed to develop object-oriented software. UML offers a modeling standard for representing software architecture.

The various elements that can be represented are :

➢ Object activity, software

➢ Players

➢ Process

➢ Database schema

---

[13] http://definition-simple.com/theorie*ds-systeme consulted on 03/02/2020 at 20:02

[14] P. Roques, *les cahiers du programmeur UML2, Modéliser une application web*, ed. Eyrolles, 4ᵉ dition, 2008, p.4

[15] http://Wikipedia.org. Accessed 03/02/2020, 16:30.

- ➢ Software component
- ➢ Component reuse

Version 2 of UML proposes thirteen diagrams that can be used to describe a system. These diagrams are grouped into two main sets.

❖ Structural diagrams: these diagrams, of which there are six, are designed to represent the static aspect of a system (class, component object, etc.).

- Class diagram: this diagram represents the static description of the system,integrating the data and processing parts of each class. It is the pivotal diagram for all system modeling.

- Object diagram: the object diagram represents an instance of a class and the links between instances.

- Component diagram: this diagram represents the different software components at system implementation level.

- Deployment diagram: this diagram describes the technical architecture of a system, focusing on the distribution of components in the operating configuration.

- Package diagram: this diagram provides an overview of the system. Structured in packages, each package represents a homogeneous set of system elements (class is component).

- Composite structure diagram: this diagram is used to describe the internal structure of a complex assembly made up, for example, of classes or objects and technical components.

❖ Behavioral diagrams: these diagrams represent the dynamic part of a system, reacting to events to produce the results expected by the user.

- Use case diagram: designed to represent the user's needs in relation to the system. It is one of the most structuring diagrams in system analysis.

- State-transition diagram: this diagram shows the different states of objects in response to events.

- Activity diagram: this diagram shows the sequence of activities specific to an operation or use case. It can also be used to represent control flows and data flows.

- Sequence diagram: this diagram describes the scenario of each use case, emphasizing the chronology of operations interacting with the objects.

- Communication diagram: this diagram is another representation of the use case scenario, focusing more on the objects and messages exchanged.

- Global interaction diagram: this diagram provides an overview of the interactions described in the sequence diagram and the control flows described in the activity diagram.

- Time diagram: this diagram represents the states and interactions of objects in a context where time has a strong influence on the behavior of the system to be managed.

- The strengths of UML[16]

UML is a formal, standardized language:

✓ precision gain

✓ a guarantee of stability

✓ Encourages the use of tools

➢ UML is a powerful communication medium, hence :

✓ It frames the analysis.

✓ It facilitates the understanding of complex abstract representations.

✓ Its versatility and flexibility make it a universal language.

✓ UML's weaknesses Putting UML into practice requires a learning curve and a period of time.

E. METHODE UP (UNIFIED PROCESS)

The complexity of computer systems has led designers to turn their attention to methods.

Object-oriented analysis methods originated in industry. The main preoccupation of their authors was software engineering, i.e. the principles and techniques needed to increase rigor and quality when building a computer application.

Initially, UML (Unified ModelingLanguage) was the result of the fusion of three object-oriented methods: the Booch method, the OMT method and the OOSE method.

In a considerable and almost miraculous event, the three "gurus" who each reigned over one of the three methods agreed to define a common method that would federate their respective contributions (they have since been dubbed "the

Amigos"). It was from this convergence effort that UML, "Unified Modeling Language", was born, the adjective "unified" being there to emphasize that UML "unifies" and therefore replaces previous methods.

The problem posed by the implementation of UML is a simple one: how do you get from the expression of requirements to the code of the application (what method do you use to get from the expression of requirements to the code of the application)? UML is only a modeling language, not a method.

---

[16] P. Roques, *Les cahiers du programmeur UML2, Modéliser une application web, Eyrolles,* 4th edition, 2008, p.4

In fact, UML does not propose a modeling approach that spells out and guides all the stages of a project, from understanding the requirements to producing the application code. A method must define a sequence of steps, partially ordered, whose objective is to produce quality software that meets users' needs within predictable times and costs.

Although UML is not a method, its authors nevertheless specify that a method based on the use of UML must be: use-case driven, architecture-centric, iterative and incremental, risk-reduction oriented[17] .

That said, among the methods using UML notation is the UP method.

UP, literally translated as "unified process", is a software development process based on UML. It is iterative, architecture-centric, use case-driven and risk-reduction oriented.

➢ **The use case-driven process,**

They provide a clear understanding of the desires and needs of future users. Use cases are not simply a tool for specifying system requirements, they will completely guide the development process through the use of models based on the UML language.

➢ **The architecture-centered process,**

This describes the different views of the system to be built. The software architecture represents the most significant static and dynamic aspects of the system. It emerges from business needs, as expressed by users and other stakeholders, and as reflected in use cases.

➢ **The iterative, incremental process**

An iteration designates the succession of stages, the sequence of activities, while an increment corresponds to an advance in the various stages of development. The iterative process limits costs, in terms of risks, to the strict expenses associated with an iteration. At each iteration, developers identify and specify the relevant use cases, create a design guided by the chosen architecture, implement this design in the form of components and check that these conform to the use cases.

➢ **The risk-reduction process**

The aim of a unified process is to control the complexity of IT projects and reduce risks.

The management of such a process is organized according to the following 4 phases: pre-study (inception), elaboration, construction and transition. Its development activities are defined by 6 fundamental disciplines: business modeling, requirements capture, analysis and

---

[17] Http// : laurent-audibert.developpez.com/Cours-UML/images consulted on 23/11/2019 at 21h30

design, implementation, testing and deployment[18].

Such a process groups together the activities required to transform a user's needs into a software system. It generally manages the following activities:

❖ **Expressing your needs :**

The expression of needs enables :
- identify the main requirements and provide a list of their functions

- identify functional requirements (from the user's point of view), leading to the development of use case models

- understand non-functional (technical) requirements and deliver a list of requirements.

The use case model presents the system from the user's point of view, and represents the customer's needs in the form of use cases and actors.

❖ **Analysis**

The aim of the analysis is to gain an understanding of the customer's needs and requirements. The aim is to produce specifications that will enable the solution to be designed.

An analysis model provides a complete specification of the requirements derived from the use cases, and structures them in a way that facilitates understanding (scenarios), preparation (architecture definition), modification and maintenance of the future system.

❖ **Design**

Design provides an in-depth understanding of the constraints associated with the programming language, component use and operating system. It determines the main interfaces and transcribes them using a common notation.

It provides a starting point for implementation:

– It breaks down the implementation work into sub-systems

– It creates a transparent abstraction of the

❖ **Implementation**

 Implementation is the result of the design to implement the system in the form of components, i.e. source code, scripts, binaries, executables and the like. The main objectives of implementation are to plan component integrations for each iteration, and to produce classes and subsystems in the form of

---

[18] P. Roque and F. Vallée, *UML2 en action, de l'analyse des besoins à la conception,* 4eme ed, EYROLLES, paris, P.24

source code.

❖ Test

Tests are used to verify the results of the implementation by testing the construction.

A methodology using UML and a set of mutually consistent best practices, it helps to circumvent the recurring problems encountered by many projects: cost and deadline drift, insufficient quality, incomplete response to user expectations. One of the strengths of this approach is its adaptability. UP can be adapted to suit the scale of a project, the experience of the team involved, and the nature of the solution to be built.

F. DATABASE MANAGEMENT SYSTEM

In computing, a database management system is a solution that enables one or more users to create and access data, and manipulate it.

A large number of DBMS exist in the management world, and we've listed some of the most popular ones below:

➢ Oracle :

Is a relational database management system which, since the introduction of object model support in version 8, can also be described as a relational database management system. There was never a version 1 for marketing reasons, the first version was version 2.

Version 3 of oracle, entirely rewritten in C programming language, in 1984 version 4 is released, in 1985 version 5, in 1988 version 6, in 1992 version 7, in 1997 version 8, in 1999 version 8i is published.

In 2001 version 9i, in 2003 version 10g, 2003 version 10g, in November 2005 version 10g express Edition, in July 2007 version 11, in September 2009, version 11g release 2 is published, and its last version was published in July 2013 is version 12c.

➢ MySQL :

MySQL is a robust and fast relational database management system (RDBMS). A database enables information to be efficiently manipulated, stored, sorted, read and searched. The MySQL server controls data access to ensure that multiple users can access the same database simultaneously and quickly, and to guarantee that only authorized users can access the data. MySQL is therefore a multi-user, multi-threaded server. It uses SQL (Structured Query Language), the standard database query language. MySQL has been available since 1996, but its development dates back to 1979. It is the most widely used open-source database in the world and has won the Linux Journal Readers' Choice Award on several occasions[19] .

---

[19] L. Welling and L. Thomson, *PHP & MYSQL*, Pearson, 4th Ed, P. 26

✓ **Some advantages of MySQL :**

MySQL's main competitors are PostgreSQL, Microsoft SQL Server and Oracle. MySQL has several advantages over them:

- high performance ;
- low cost ;

-easy to set up and learn;

- portability ;
- accessibility of its source code;
- support availability.

MySQL is undeniably a fast system[20] .

Most tests show that MySQL is several orders of magnitude faster than its competitors. In 2002, eWeek published a test bench comparing five databases powering a web application. The best result was a tie between MySQL and Oracle, even though Oracle is a much more expensive product.

-Reduced cost

MySQL is available free of charge under an open-source license or, for a very reasonable price, under a commercial license. You'll need to purchase a license if you want to redistribute MySQL in an application and don't want the application to be under an open-source license. If you don't intend to distribute your application (which is generally the case with most web applications) or if you're working on open-source software, you don't need to buy a license.

- Easy to use

Most modern databases use SQL.

MySQL is easier to install than most similar products. The learning curve required to become a DataBase Administrator (DBA) is much shorter than for other databases.

-Portability

MySQL can be used on a large number of Unix systems, as well as with Windows.

-Source code

As with PHP, you can obtain the MySQL source code from

Support availability

Not every open-source product has a parent company offering support, training, consulting and certification services: you can get all this from MySQL AB (www.mysql.com).

---

[20] http://web.mysql.com/why-mysql/benchmark.html. Accessed on 03/02/2020 22:20

CHAPTER TWO PRELIMINARY ANALYSIS

II.1 INTRODUCTION

The preliminary analysis stage in an IT project mainly consists of taking stock of the IT solutions already implemented in the company, and identifying requirements, particularly in terms of new functionalities.

II .2 SYSTEM DELIMITATION

II.2.1   PRESENTATION OF THE ORGANIZATION

a.   *Name*

The scope of our study is the urban sub-division of EPST/LIKASI1.

b.   *Geographical location*

Our studies were carried out in the urban sub-division of EPST/ LIKASI I, located in the commune of LIKASI and in the town of the same name. At the corner of avenues JACARANDA, de l'indépendance and boulevard kamanyola, within the Mapinduzi school complex. It is located 400 metres from the Sainte-Thérèse Catholic Church and diagonally across from Likasi city park.

c.   *Historical overview*

The LIKASI sub-division was created by ministerial decree in 1975. In 2018, it will be split into two separate subdivisions, LIKASI 1 and LIKASI 2.

LIKASI 1 manages the communes of Likasi, SHITURU and PANDA, while the commune of KIKULA is managed by LIKASI2.

d.   *STATUS AND PURPOSE*

1.   *Legal status*
The EPST/LIKASI sub-division is a state institution supervised by the LUBUMBASHI provincial division at provincial level and by the Ministry dEPST at national level.

2.   *Objective*
The management of a Sub-Division of Primary, Secondary and Vocational Education is essentially focused on the administrative, pedagogical and financial supervision of public and private school staff, in line with the official directives and instructions in force.

e. ***ORGANIZATION AND OPERATION***

1. ***Administrative organization***
The Subdivision office is organized administratively into 17 cells/departments coordinated by the Subdivision Chief:

1. Office of the Subdivision Manager

2. Secretariat

3. General services

4. Accounting

5. O.S.P (Orientation Scolaire et Professionnel)

6. School planning and statistics

7. Educational

8. Technical education and training

9. E.V.F/EMP (Education for life and family)

10. Pensions and survivors' benefits

11. Special education

12. School infrastructure

13. Cultures and school sports

14. E.P.A (Approved Private School)

15. School partnership

16. Nursery and primary education

17. Secondary education

2. How it works :
1. The Sub-Proved: is the authority who commits and supervises the cells/departments of the sub-division. During the course of the year, he is responsible for various activities such as administration, pedagogy, socio-cultural activities, finance and infrastructure.

2. Secretariat: its role is to receive mail and visitors, process mail and referrals, type and file

documents.

3.   General services: centralizes information on the careers of the entity's personnel
; coordinates and processes the entity's personnel management activities.

4.   O.S.P. (Orientation Scolaire et Professionnel): its role is to :

-   Supervising COSPs assigned to schools ;

-   Supervise activities related to school guidance ;

-   Monitoring students' academic progress and organizing tests ;

-   Psychological support for students.

5.   School planning and statistics: this department is responsible for :

-   Annual census of nursery, primary, secondary and technical schools to update the school
map;

-   School viability survey, prior to school promotion notice;

-   Preparation for the sectoral school promotion and transmission of data to the provincial
school promotion meetings;

-   Preparation of the school directory as raw data.

6.   Special education: the remit of this unit/service is to identify and monitor establishments
offering special education; recovery centers, remedial education centers, schools for the deaf
and schools for the physically handicapped.

7.   Pensions and survivors' pensions: pensions and survivors' pensions play an important
role in education:

-   identification of deceased teachers ;

-   retractable teacher identification via payroll listings ;

-   census of sick teachers ;
-   management of social cases in accordance with letter N°MINEPSP/KE/081/850/2009
entrusting this prerogative to the unit.

8.   E.V.F/EMP (Education for Family Life): this is responsible for training educators in
education for life and registering candidates for training; it also recruits teachers and training

supervisors.

9. Infrastructure: manages :

- infrastructure inventory ;

- collection and processing of equipment requirements and the construction or rehabilitation of school infrastructures.

10. Partenariat Scolaire: this unit deals with collaboration with educational partners and NGOs involved in the EPST sector, for actions in favor of education.

11. school culture and sport: oversees and facilitates the popularization, promotion, regulation, organization, coordination and control of cultural and sporting activities in primary and secondary schools.

12. Teaching unit: the teaching unit aims to :

- organization, planning and control of educational activities in LIKASI schools;

- ensures compliance with teaching instructions;

- exploits the various reports.

13. Private education: Manages the pedagogical, administrative and financial aspects of private schools.

14. Enseignement Technique: Responsible for all schools that organize technical sections.

15. Accounting: Responsible for staff payroll, managing financial documents and dealing with unpaid bills.

General organization chart

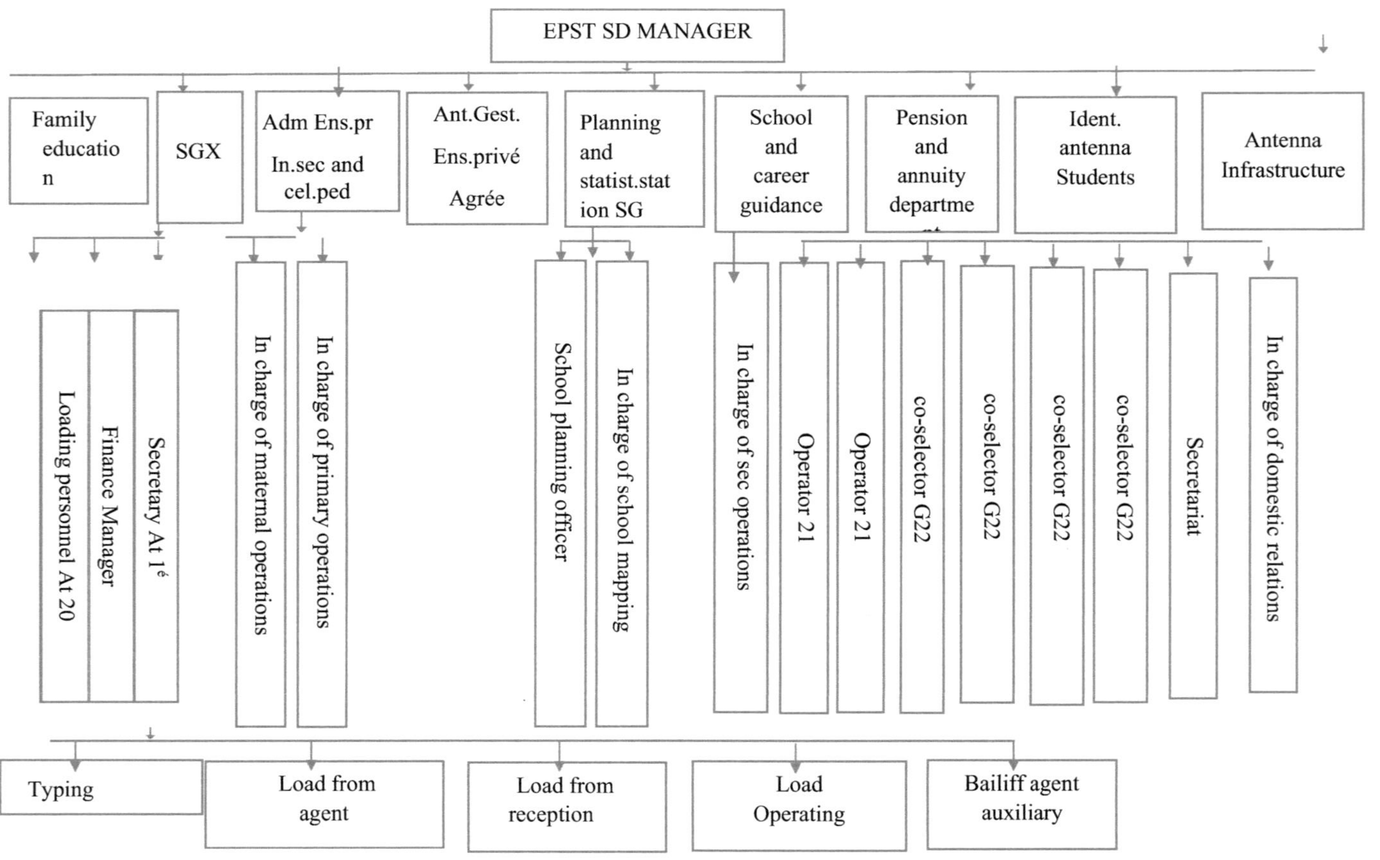

Source: EPST/Likasi secretariat as of 10/10/2020

26

SERNIE ORGANIZATION

The SERNIE of the EPST/LIKASI sub-division is organized as follows next :

➢ The department manager (cell manager) ;
➢ Operators ;
➢ Collectors ;

II.2.2   DESCRIPTION OF EXISTING

a.   CRITICISM OF EXISTING SYSTEMS

➢ The organization's administrative tasks and procedures relating to student follow-up are manual, making the task complex and time-consuming.

➢ Difficulty in monitoring: it's difficult for the SERNIE manager to keep track of work progress and control task completion.

➢ Poor information storage: the same information is stored several times on all workstations. The problem posed is therefore one of redundancy of the same information, so that any change to it at one workstation is not directly reflected at the other workstations.

II.2.2.3   PROPOSED SOLUTION

The proposed solution to the current process problems is to automate some of the sub-division's tasks using a web application.

II.2.2.4   STATIC CONTEXT DIAGRAM

The static context diagram is used to specify the number of actor instances connected to the system at a given time [21] . This diagram can be drawn using a class diagram involving only the actors and the system.

---

[21] P. Roques & F. vallée, ibidem, P 64.

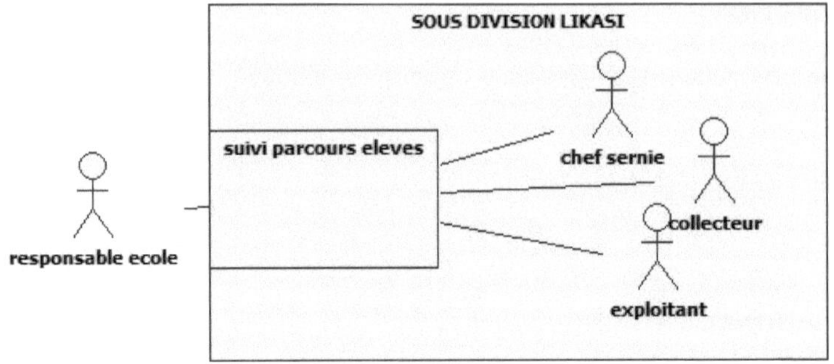

Figure 1: Static context diagram

II.3.2 Business use case diagram

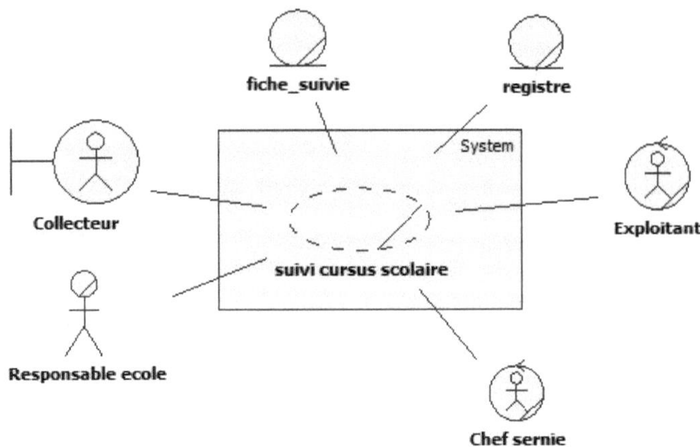

Figure 2: Business use case diagram

II.2.2.5   BUSINESS PROCESS ANALYSIS

A business process, also known as a business process or enterprise process, refers to a set of interrelated or interacting activities that contribute to an organization's business goals[22] . The business process is executed by human actors or by automata using resources. In UML, these processes are represented using activity diagrams.

---

[22] http://fr .m.wikipedia.org/wiki/business_processes. Accessed on 26/02/2020 at 11h57

Tracking a student's progress

At the start of each new year, collectors visit the city's schools to gather information on the pupils enrolled. The head of the school draws up an identification register, a copy of which is given to the collectors. The collectors in turn pass it on to the operators, who compile the data and present it to the SERNIE manager. The identities of pupils at each school are recorded in a register.

At the end of the year, collectors return to the schools. This time, the person in charge of the school draws up a follow-up sheet for each pupil, which includes the pupil's identity (previous class, next class, decision, etc.). After collection, these forms are forwarded to the operators, who compile them and report back to the SERNIE manager.

Activity diagram

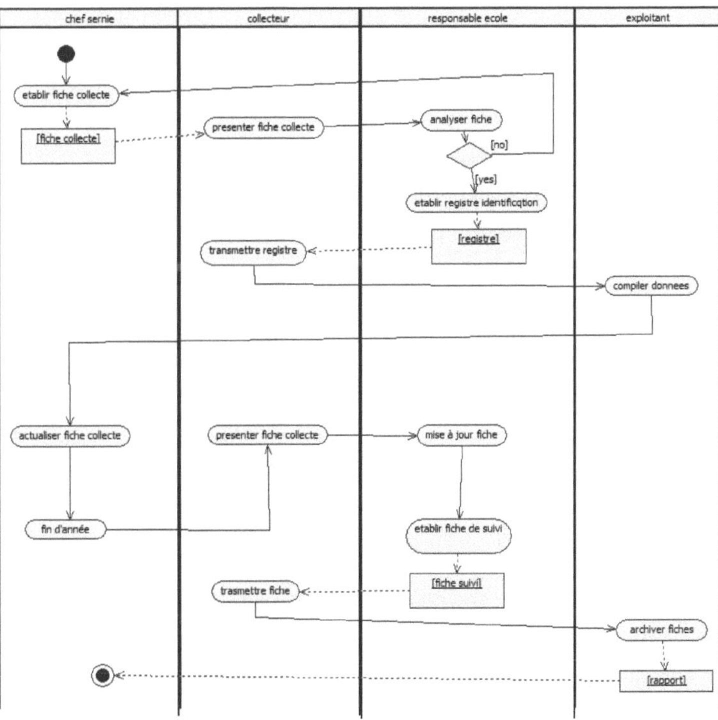

Figure 3: Monitoring process activity diagram

II.3.DETERMINATION OF USE CASES

II.3.1   IDENTIFICATION OF STAKEHOLDERS AND USE CASES

➢ Identifying the players

An actor represents the abstraction of a role played by external entities (user or other system) that interact directly with the system under study[23] .

• **The collector:** his role is to go out into the field. In other words, they go into the various schools to gather information about the pupils.

• **The** operator is responsible for compiling the information gathered by the collectors and reporting to the SERNIE manager.

• **The Head of SERNIE** is an actor whose role is to codify the students.

• **The school manager:** this is a school director who

benefits from SERNIE services. He can be a director, a prefect, ...

➢ Determining use cases

Use cases describe, in the form of actions, the behavior of a system from the user's point of view. They are used to structure user requirements and the corresponding system objectives. Given the above requirements, we have identified the following use cases:

❖ Sign in

❖ Create school account

❖ Update prize list: update the prize list.

❖ See the awards

❖ Ask for student transfer

❖ Process request Transfer

II.3.2.   TEXTUAL DESCRIPTION OF USE CASES

The textual description of the use cases is especially detailed in order to obtain a precise expression of requirements. Each use case must be associated with a textual description of the iterations between the actors and the system. This is divided into six points:

Objective: is a succinct description of the context and expected results of case studies[24] .

---

[23] P.Roques and F.vallee ; opcit ; p51

[24] J.Gabay et D.Gabay, *UML2 Analyse et conception*, Ed Dunod, paris, 2008, p82

- **Actors involved**: whether primary or secondary, the actors involved in the use case must be identified, specifying their overall role.
- **Precondition**: if certain conditions are required before the case can be executed, they must be stated at this level.
- **Nominal scenario**: this is the main accident-free scenario that leads to the desired result.
- **Alternative scenarios**: these are variants of the secondary scenario.
- **Post condition**: at this level, certain specific conditions must be met after the case has been executed.

1) Update prize list

➢ **Purpose:** this use case enables the operator to perform certain operations to update the prize list. The operations supported are: adding, modifying and deleting student information from the ranking list.

➢ **Main actor:** operator

➢ **Precondition:** -

➢ **Nominal scenario :**

Operator	System
1. Request for prize list form	2. Displays the form

Alternative scenario

a. Case of an addition

1. The operator requests the add-on form
2. the system displays the requested form
3. the operator enters information about a student
4. validates the entry
5. the system saves and displays a confirmation message

b. Case of a modification

1. Operator requests modification form
2. the system displays the requested form
3. the operator initiates a search for the follow-up sheet
4. the system searches for the student
5. the operator enters the changes to be made
6. validates the entry
7. the system modifies and displays a confirmation message

c. Case of deletion

1. Operator requests deletion form

2. The system displays the requested form

3. The operator selects the student

4. It validates the deletion

5. The system deletes the pensioner and displays a confirmation message

2) See awards

Purpose: this use case enables a system user to consult the students' ranking.

➢ **The key player: the** user

➢ **Precondition:** existence o f   at least one follow-up sheet in the

➢ **Nominal scenario :**

User	System
1. Request the prize list consultation form	Display form
3. Select a student	5. searches for and displays the page corresponding to the student's ranking.
4. Confirm selection	

➢ **Post condition: -**

3) Request transfer

Purpose: this use case allows the head of a school to request the transfer of a student to another school.

➢ **The key player: the** school manager.

➢ **Precondition:** existence of the school and student account in the system.

➢ Nominal scenario :

School manager	System
1. Request the transfer request form	2. Displays the requested form
3. Edit request	5. sends the request and displays a confirmation message
4. It validates the dispatch of the request	

➢ Post condition: existence of a new request in the system.

4) Process transfer request

Purpose: this use case enables the SERNIE manager to validate or invalidate a request to transfer a given pupil to another school.

➢ **Lead actor:** chef SERNIE

➢ **Precondition:** at least one application waiting to be processed.

➢ **Nominal scenario :**

Chef SERNIE	System
1. Request processing form requests	2. Displays the form
3. Start request search	5. search and display request
4. He validates the request	6. displays a confirmation message

➢ Alternative scenario :

a. Rejection of request

1. the SERNIE chief rejects the request

2. the system displays a confirmation message

➢ Post condition: change in application status.

5) Sign in

Purpose: this use case enables a user to access a system after entering his or her identity.

➢ **The key player: the** user

➢ **Precondition:** existence o f at least one user account, i.e. login and password on the system.

➢ **Nominal scenario :**

User	System
1. Request identification form	2. displays the form
3. Enter login and password pass	5. verifies login and password and displays the main menu by opening a new session
4. Starts the opening request of its session.	

- ➤ **Alternative scenario**

a.   Entering incorrect identities

a.1   the system returns an error message and the nominal scenario resumes at scenario step 3.

- ➤ **Post condition:** new user session.

6)   Create school account

Purpose: this use c a s e enables the SERNIE manager to create an account for each school whose pupils he or she monitors.

- ➤ **Lead actor:** chef SERNIE

- ➤ **Precondition:** no school account in the system.

- ➤ **Nominal scenario :**

Chef SERNIE	System
1. Request school account creation form	2. Poster the form requested
3. Enter information from account	5. creates the account and displays a confirmation message
4. Ilvalide creation from account	

- ➤ Post condition: existence of a new school account in the system.

II. 3.3 USE CASE DIAGRAM

Use case diagrams are UML diagrams used to give an overall view of the functional behavior of a software system.

For the sake of readability, we have shown the functional use case diagram and the technical use case diagram separately.

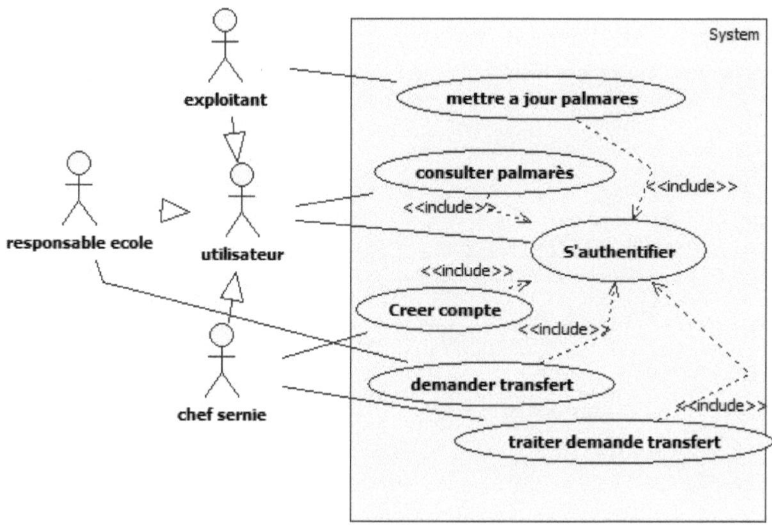

Figure 4: Use case diagram

II.4.   SYSTEM SEQUENCE DIAGRAM

Sequence diagram: "Authenticate yourself

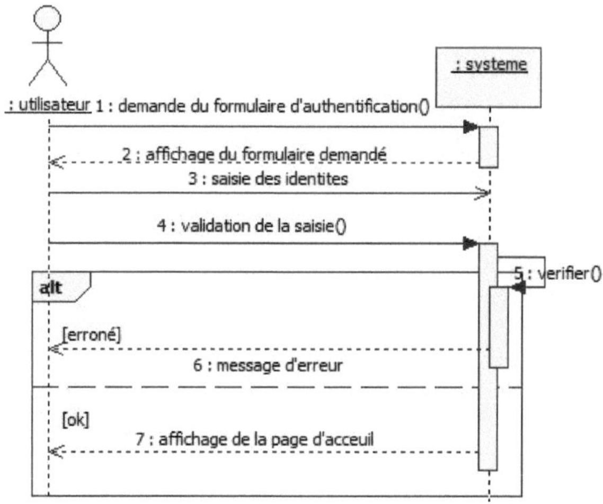

Figure 5: authentication sequence diagram

Create school account" sequence diagram

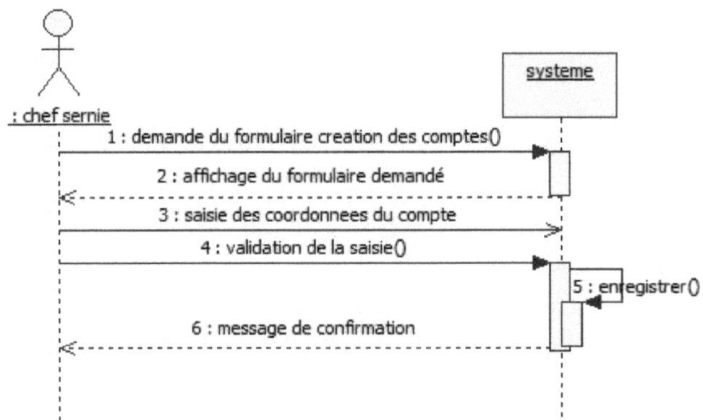

Figure 6: Create account sequence diagram

Palmarès update" sequence diagram

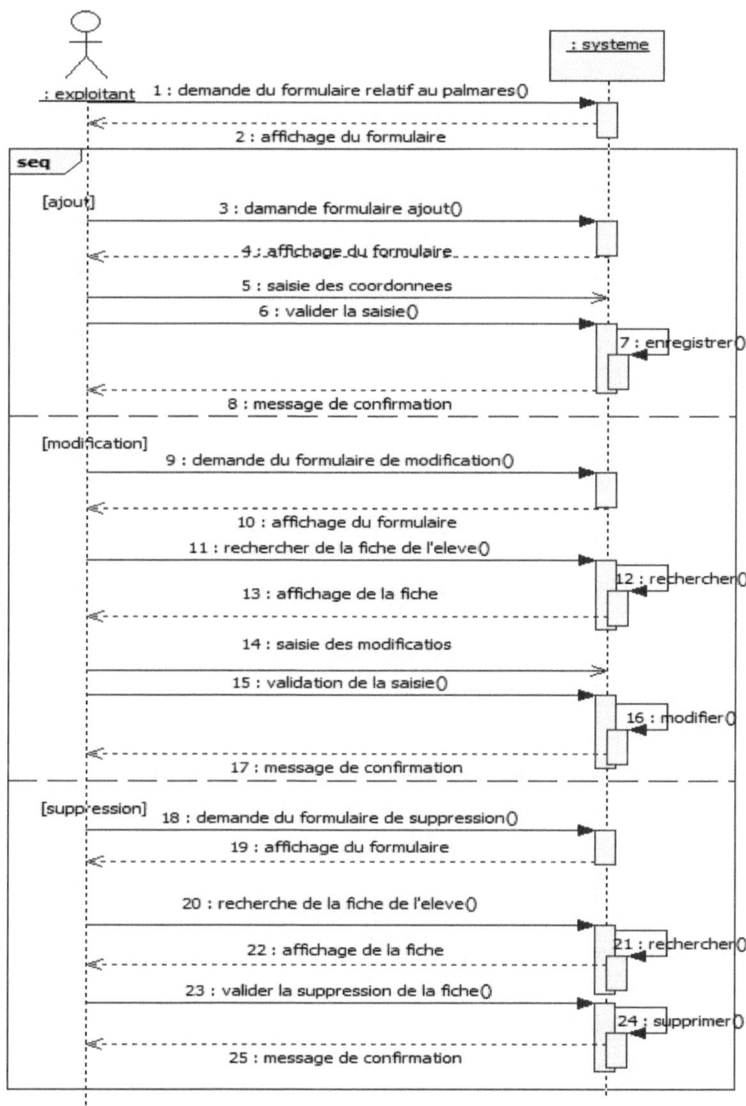

Figure 7: Create account sequence diagram

Consult prize list" sequence diagram

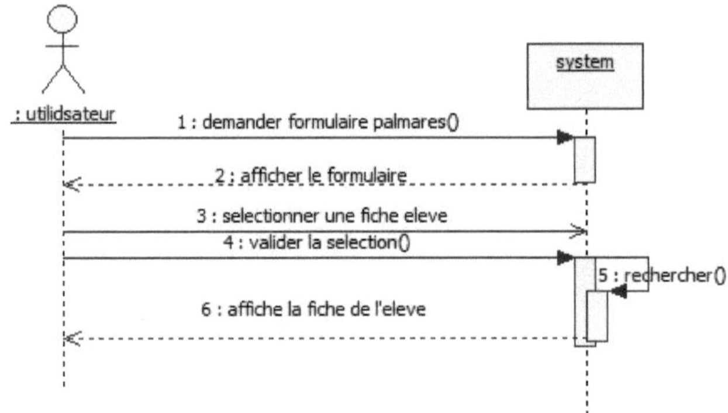

Figure 8: Sequence diagram for consulting the prize list

Request transfer" sequence diagram

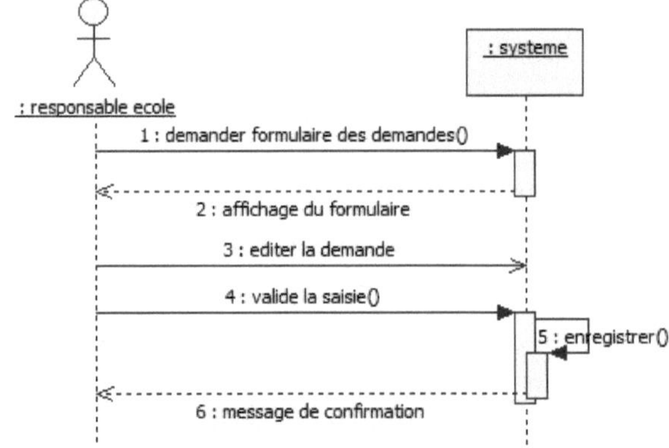

Figure 9: sequence diagram request transfer

Process transfer request" sequence diagram

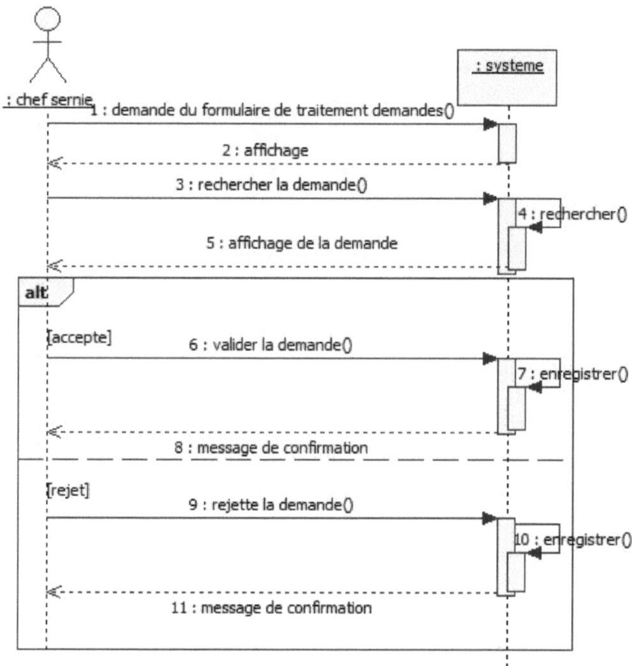

Figure 10: Processing transfer request sequence diagram

II.5. DOMAIN CLASS DIAGRAM

The class diagram is considered the most important element of object-oriented modeling. It provides an abstract representation of the system objects that will interact to realize the use cases. It's important to note that the same object may well be involved in the realization of several use cases.

The domain class diagram generally represents the static structure of a system in terms of classes. Its role is to represent a set of objects, while a relationship or association is used to show the links between these objects.

II.5.1 IDENTIFICATION OF DOCUMENTS USED

In this section, we identify the different media involved in the process, in order to highlight the classes in the field.

a.   Pupil register: this is a document in which the pupils of each school are recorded.

Pupil number, pupil's name, post name, first name, date of birth, gender, pupil's place of birth, nationality, date of enrolment, class, option, pupil's address, school year.

b.   Tracking form: this is a form used to track a student's progress through the sub-division each year.

Pupil number, pupil name, post name, first name, date of birth, gender, pupil's place of birth, nationality, enrolment date, class, option, next class, previous class, percentage, decision, school name, school address, school year.

c.   Fiche de mouvement: this is a document certifying the transfer of a pupil from one school to another.

Pupil number, pupil name, post name, first name, date of birth, gender, place of birth, nationality, date of enrolment, class, option, name of sending school, destination school, reason for transfer.

II.5.2   CLASS DIAGRAM

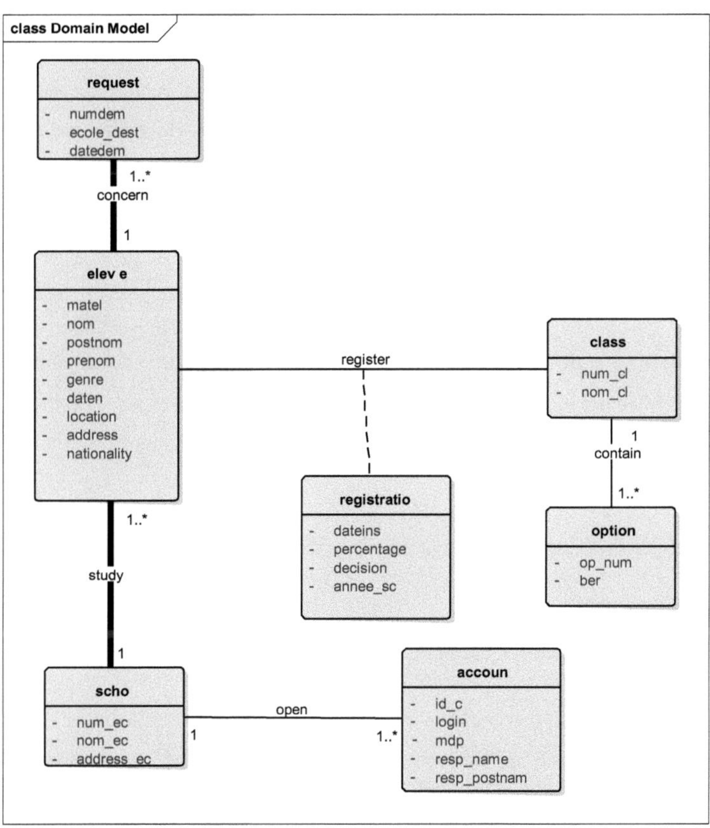

Figure 11: Domain class diagram

CHAPTER THREE E
DETAILED DESIGN OF THE COMPUTER SYSTEM

III.1   INTRODUCTION

This is the most common type of data model used to create a database. According to this type of model, the database is made up of a set of tables (relationships) in which data and links are placed.

III.2   PRELIMINARY DESIGN

III.2.1   SOFTWARE ARCHITECTURE

A software architecture is the way in which the various elements of a computer system are organized. The architecture model produced during the design phase does not describe what a computer system should achieve, but rather how it should be designed to meet user specifications[25] .

Analysis describes the "what to do", while architecture describes the "how to do it".
do "

In our case, we have chosen the MVC (Model-View-Controller) architecture.

MVC is an architecture model that seeks to clearly separate the presentation layer (UI: User Interface), the business layer (BLL: Business Logic Layer) and the data access layer (DAL: Data Access Layer). The aim is to have minimal dependency between the different layers of the application, so that modifications made on any layer of the application do not affect the other layers[26] .

The model layer represents the part of the application that executes the business logic. This means that it is responsible for retrieving data, converting it into meaningful concepts for the application, such as processing, validation, association and many other data manipulation tasks.

At first glance, the Model object can be seen as the first layer of interaction with any database

---

[25] En.m.wikipedia.org/wiki/Architecture_logicielle. Accessed on 09/05/2020

[26] www.fr.wikipédia.com consulted on 03/04/2020

in the application. But more globally, it is one of the major concepts around which the application is executed.

The view returns a presentation of data from the model. Separated by the Model Objects, it is responsible for using the information available to it to produce a presentation interface for the application.

For example, just as the Model layer returns a set of data, the View uses this data to provide an HTML page. Or a formatted XML output. The Vue layer isn't just limited to HTML or text representation of data. It can also be used to provide a wide variety of formats to suit your needs, such as video, music, documents and any other format you can think of.

The control layer manages user requests. It is responsible for returning a response with the mutual help of the Model and View layers.

Controllers can be imagined as managers whose job it is to check that all the resources required to complete a task are delegated to workers in the right way. They wait for requests from clients, check their validity according to authentication and authorization rules, delegate the data retrieved and processed by the Model and select the correct presentation types that the client accepts, finally delegating the display process to the View layer.

❖   illustration of the MVC model :

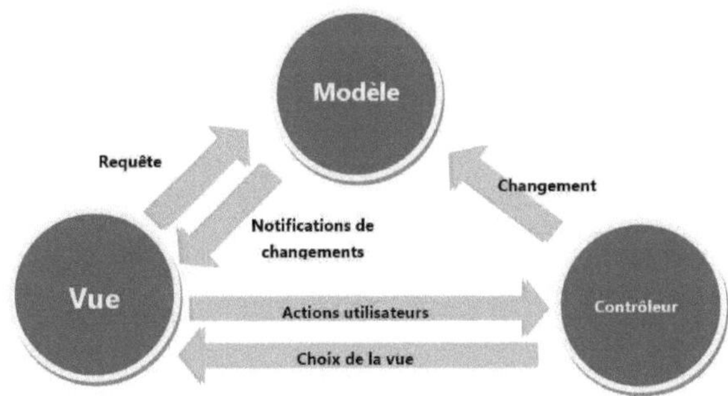

Figure 12: MVC model

III.2.1.1 Different use case interfaces

➢ Create a school account

➢ Update prize list

➢ Request student transfer

➢ Processing the transfer request

III.2.2.1. Iterations and system operations

In this section, the use cases (iterations) are represented, i.e., one use case is realized after another, in order to deduce the participating class diagram and the detailed sequence diagram for each use case.

An iteration is a succession of steps within a project.

1. Create school account
2. Update prize list
- Add student information
- Find information about a student
- Modify student information
- Delete student information.
3. Request transfer
- Search student
- Create request
4. Process transfer request
- Validate request
- Reject request

III.2.2.2. Design class diagram

a. Create school account" design class diagram

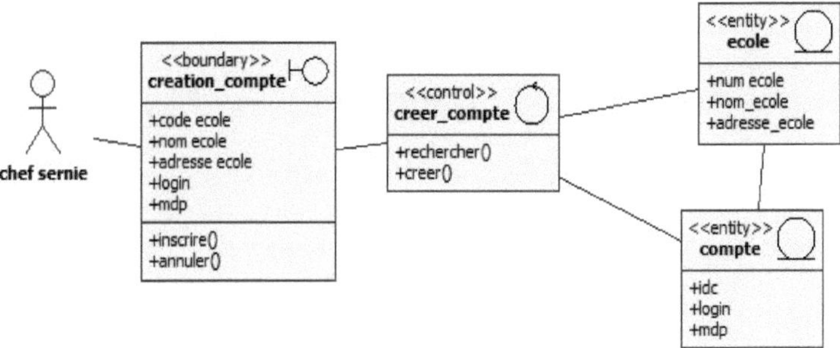

Figure 13: diagram of participating class create school account

b. Class diagram of the "update prize list" design

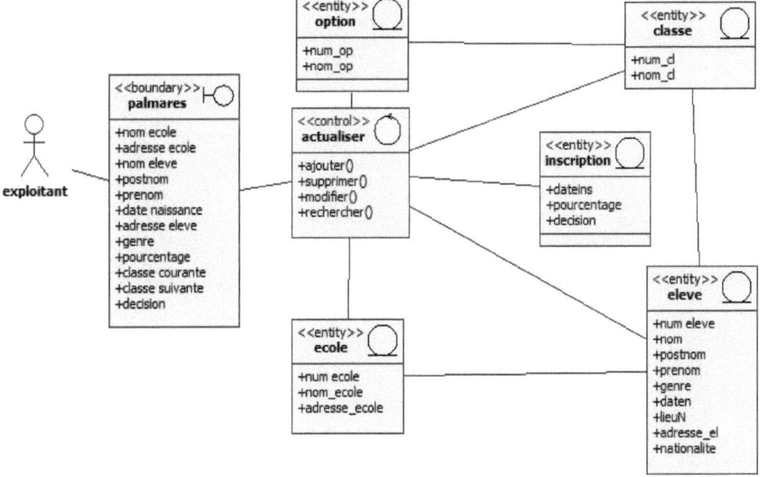

Figure 14: Participant class diagram - update ranking list

c. Request transfer" design class diagram

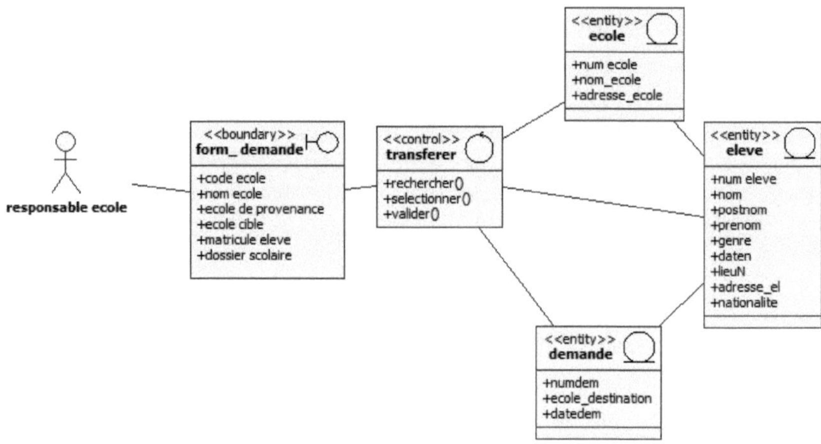

Figure 15: Participating class diagram request transfer

d. Process transfer request" design class diagram

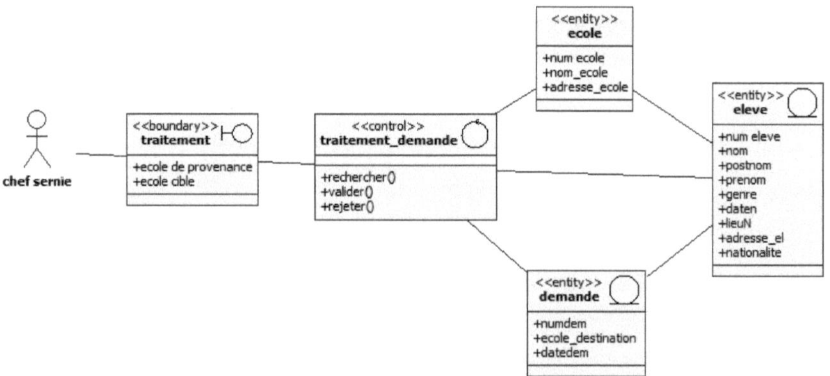

Figure 16: Participant class diagram: process transfer request

III.2.2.3. detailed sequence diagram

a.   Create school account" detailed sequence diagram

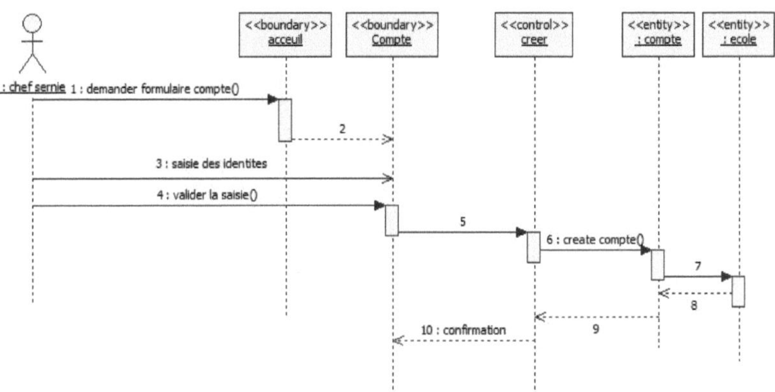

Figure 17: detailed sequence diagram create account

b.   Detailed sequence diagram for "update prize list".

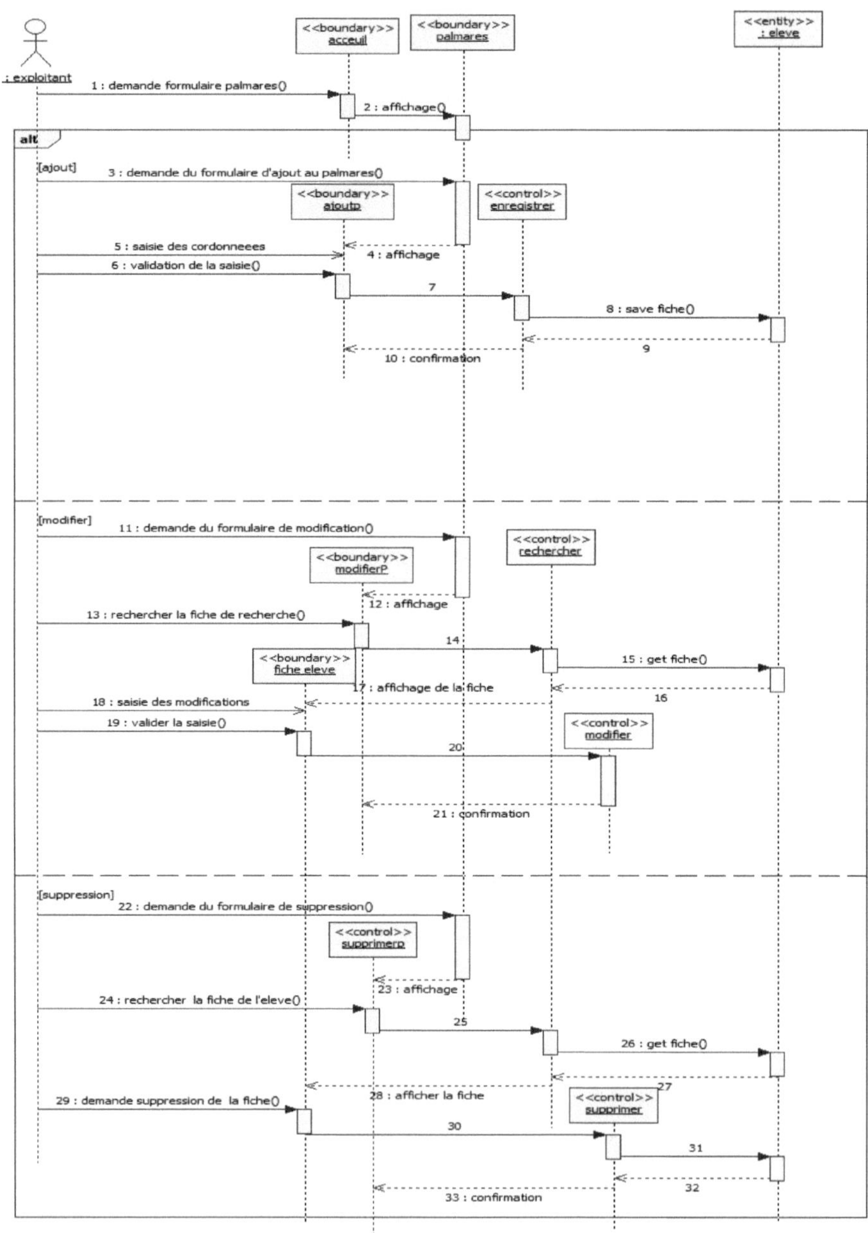

Figure 18: detailed sequence diagram: update catalog

c. See awards

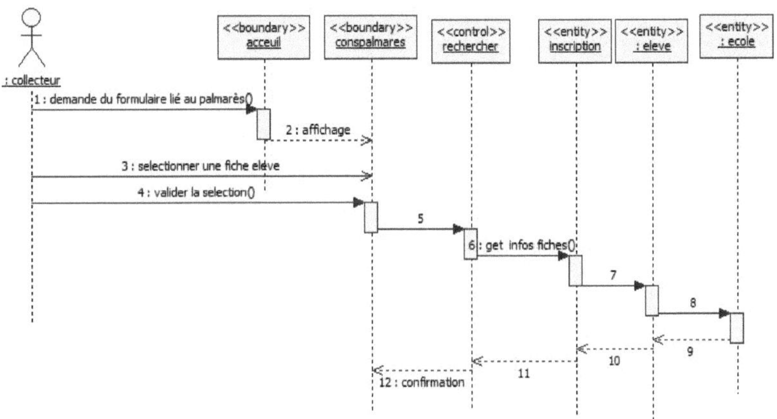

Figure 19: Detailed sequence diagram, consult ranking list

d. Request transfer" detailed sequence diagram

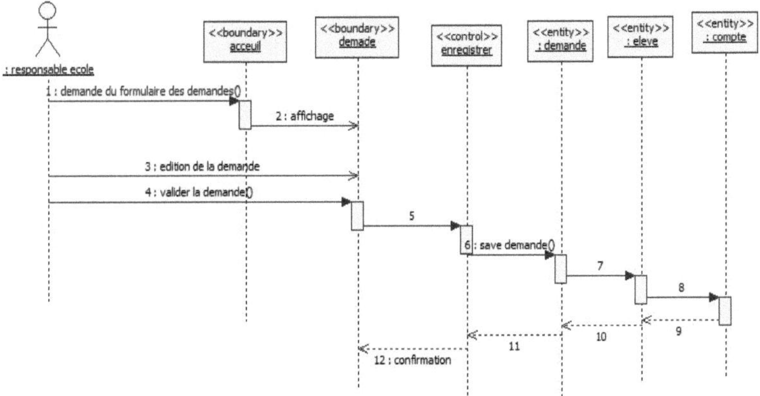

Figure 20: detailed sequence diagram request transfer

e.   Process transfer request" detailed sequence diagram

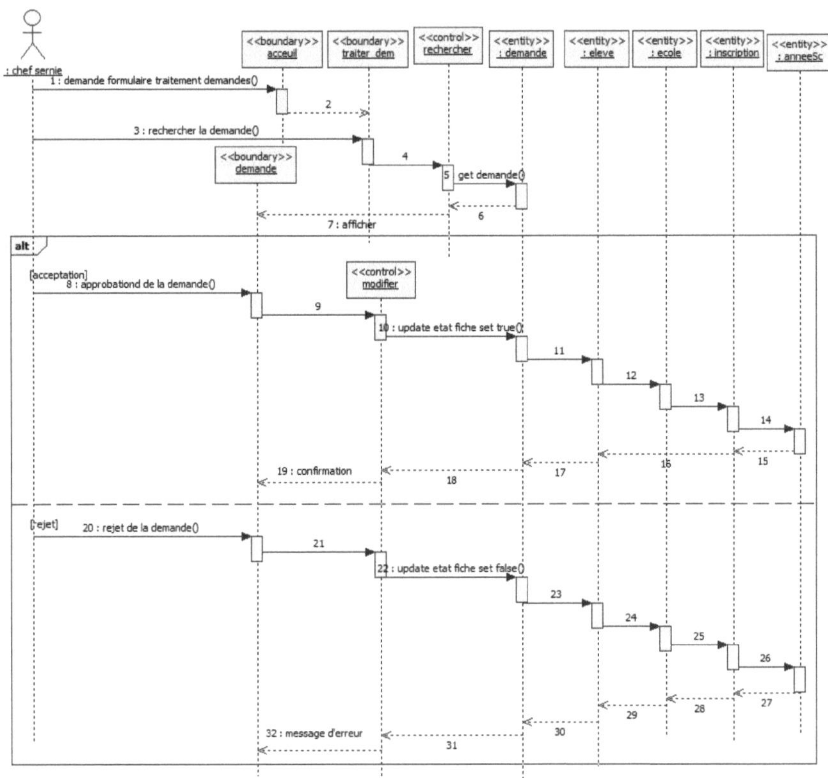

Figure 21: detailed sequence diagram processing request

III.3. DETAILED DESIGN

III.3.1 DATA LOGIC MODEL

The relational model allows us to reformulate the conceptual model in a formalism much closer to IT implementation, although still independent of any particular technological solution.

As the conceptual model is a formal model, the logical model is also intended to be a formal model, but no longer specifying the existing or desired reality as in the conceptual model, but the data as it will exist in the IT application.

For this reason, a few transformation rules need to be observed in order to move from the conceptual model to the relational model.

III.3.1.1 Rules for moving from conceptual to relational models

This is the most common type of data model used to create a database. According to this type of model, the database is made up of a set of tables (relationships) in which data and links are placed.

a) Class transformation :
For each class in the conceptual model, a table (relationship) is created in the relational model, and a class attribute must be chosen to play the role of primary key. If no attribute is suitable for this role, an additional attribute must be added to fill this role. Except in the case of inheritance, where the attributes of the table in question can be combined to form a table. The properties of the class become the attributes of the table. In the case o f a strong class, its identifier becomes the table key.

b) Transformation of associations :
➢ Association classes :

In the case of an association class, the corresponding table will have as its key an obligatory key composed of all the identifiers of the classes participating in the association, and each attribute of the composed key also plays the role of foreign key.

➢ Binary associations (one-to-many): for this type of association, a foreign key attribute must be added to the child relationship (class with maximum cardinality "*") of the association. The attribute is named after the key of the association's parent relationship.
➢ One-to-one association :
For this type, a foreign key attribute must be added to the relationship derived from the class with a minimum multiplicity of one. The attribute is named after the primary key of the relationship derived from the class connected to the association.

In fact, the application of these rules has led to the creation of the following relationship diagram:

-    School (<u>school_number</u>,school_name,school_address)
-    Eleve(<u>matel</u>,nom,postnom,prenom,genre,daten,lieun,adressel,nation nalite,num_ec#)
-    demandet(<u>numdem</u>,ecole_dest,datedem, matel#)

-    Class(<u>_num_cl</u>,nom_cl)
-    Inscription(<u>matel#,num_cl#,num_annee#</u>,dateins,pourcentage,decisi on,annee_sc)

- Option(<u>op_number,</u>op_name,cl#_number)
- Account(<u>id_c,</u>login, mdp,nom_resp,postnom_resp,num_ec#)

III.3.1.2 PHYSICAL DATA MODEL

- Create database palmares ;
- Create table ecole(num_ec char(10) primary key, nom_ec char(15),adresse_ec(25)) ;
- Create table eleve(matel varchar(15),nom varchar(20),postnom varchar(20),prenom varchar(20),genre varchar(10),daten date,lieun varchar(15),adresseel varchar(20),nationnalite varchar(20),num_ec varchar(10), foreign key references ecole(num_ec)) ;
- Create table demande(numdem int primary key,ecole_dest varchar(10),datedem date matel varchar(10),foreign key references eleve(matel));
- Create table Classe(num_cl int primary key,nom_cl varchar(10))
- Create table Inscription(matel varchar(10),num_cl int,num_annee int,dateins date, primary key (matel,num_cl,num_annee),foreign key(matel)references eleve(matel), foreign key(num_cl)references classe(num_cl),   foreign   key(num_annee)   references anneesc(num_annee), pourcentage int, annee_sc date, decision varchar(10));
- Create table Option(num_op int primary key,nom_op varchar(15),num_cl int, foreign key(num_cl)references classe(num_cl))
- Create table Compte(id_c int primary key,login varchar(20), mdp varchar(15),nom_resp varchar(20),postnom_resp   varchar(20),num_ec   varchar(10),   foreign key(num_ec)references ecole(num_ec))

CHAPTER FOUR
IMPLEMANTATION AND DEPLOYMENT OF THE SOFTWARE SOLUTION

III.1 INTRODUCTION

In this chapter, we define the development tools used to implement our application. Then we present some of the application's interfaces and source code.

III.2 Web application

A web application is a software application hosted on a server and accessible via a web browser. Unlike traditional software, users of a web application do not need to install it on their computer. They simply connect to the application via their browser.

III.3 ADVANTAGES OF A WEB APPLICATION

1. Universal access from any type of workstation: PC, laptop, cell phone, tablet;
2. No operating system incompatibility (all you need is a browser);
3. Work from anywhere in the world;
4. Data are centralized ;
5. Data is available 24 hours a day, 7 days a week;
6. No risk of data loss.

III.4 DEVELOPMENT TOOLS :

a. Diagram development :

To create the UML diagrams used to model our web application, we used diagram development software:

STAR UML is a Unified Modeling Language (UML) tool and code generator.

It can create diagrams o f software and other systems in the industry-standard UML format, and can also generate code from UML diagrams in a variety of programming languages.

b. PhpMyAdmin :

PhpMyAdmin is a free software tool written in PHP, designed to manage MySQL administration on the Web. PhpMyAdmin supports a wide range of MySQL and MariaDB operations.

Frequently used operations (managing databases, tables, columns, relationships, indexes, users, authorizations, etc.) can be performed via the user interface, while you always have the option of executing a SQL statement directly.

c. MYSQL :

MySQL is a free relational database first launched in 1995 and widely used on the Web, often in conjunction with PHP (language) and Apache (web server). MySql runs on all operating systems (including Windows, Linux and Mac OS). The principle of a relational database is to store information in tables, which represent groups of data by subject (product table, user table, etc.) Tables are linked together by relationships.

d. Mozilla Firefox :

Mozilla Firefox is a free, open-source web browser, developed and distributed by the Mozilla Foundation with the help of thousands of volunteers using open source development methods and free source code.

3.5) Programming language :

3.5.1)   PHP :

PHP is a recursive acronym that stands for PHP: Hypertext Preprocessor. It is a language embedded in HTML and interpreted or compiled on the server side. It is derived from C and Perl, whose syntax it adopts.

This language is mainly used to produce dynamic websites. It is common for this language to be associated with a database, such as MySQL.

Running on the server side (where the site is hosted), visitors don't need any special software or plug-ins.

Since it supports all web standards and is free of charge, it has spread rapidly across the web. PHP can be installed on all major web servers on the market.

III.5 DEPLOYMENT MODEL

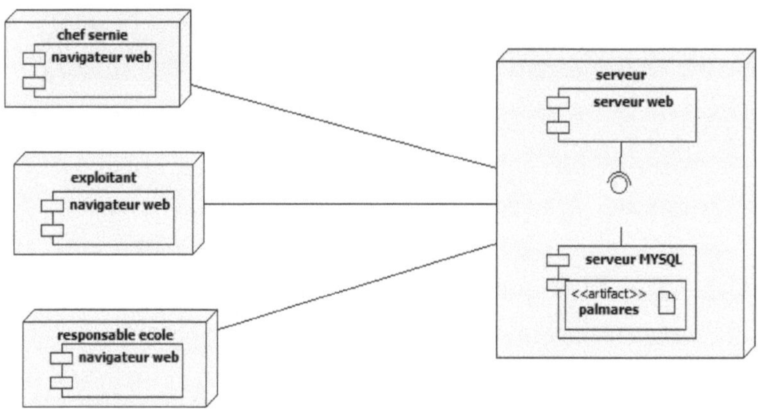

Figure 22: deployment diagram

IV.6. PROGRAMMING AND INTERFACE PRESENTATION

a. INTERFACE PRESENTATION

1. Authentication interface

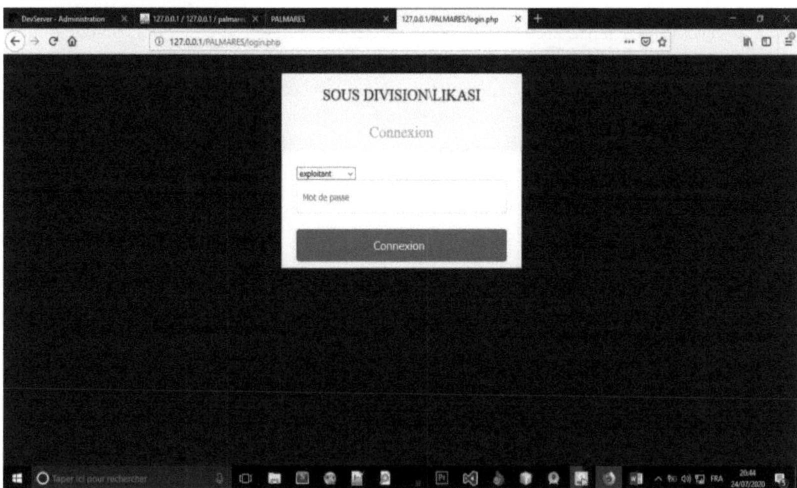

Figure 23: authentication interface

2. Operator interface

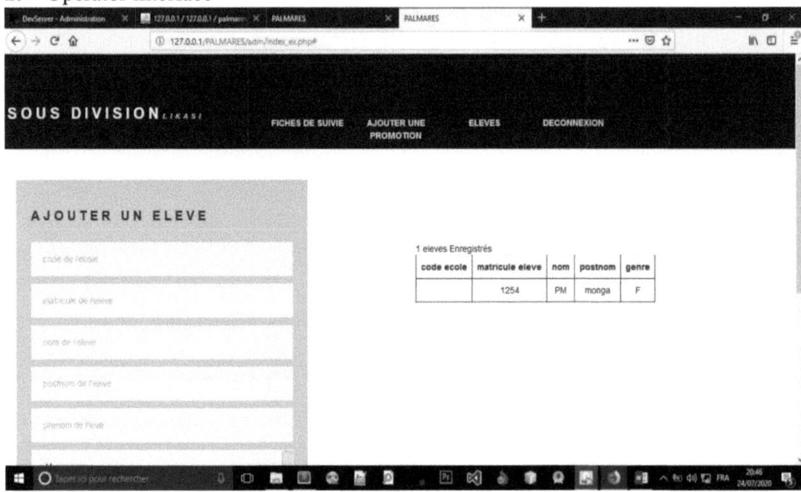

code ecole	matricule eleve	nom	postnom	genre
	1254	PM	monga	F

Figure 24: operator interface

3. Interface chef SERNIE

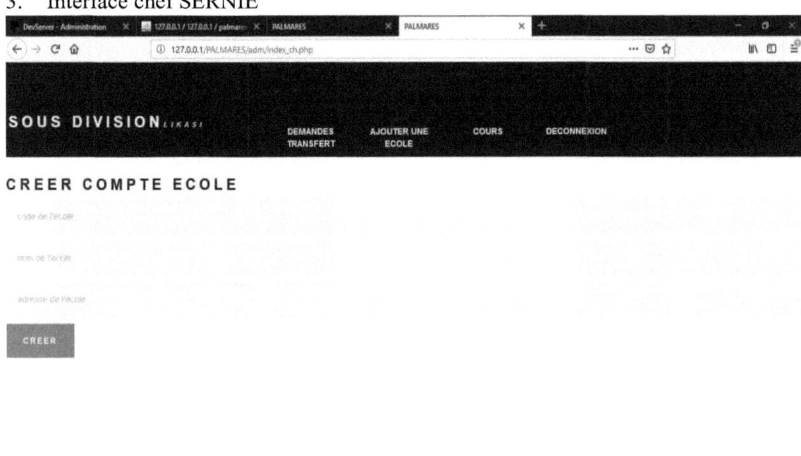

Figure 25: serialized chef interface

4. Awards interface

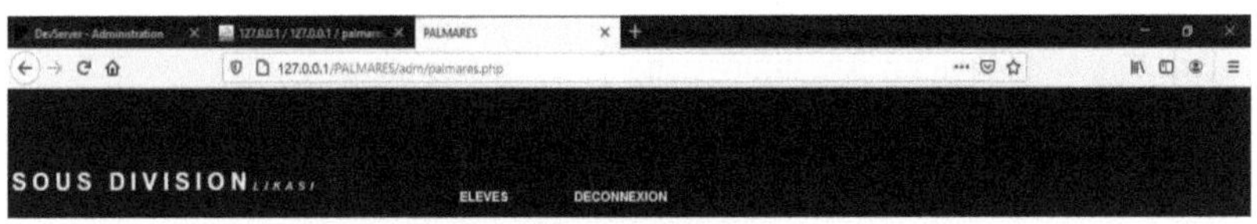

code ecole	matricule eleve	classe courante	classe suivante	pourcentage	decision	annee scolaire	action
e002	el02	2eme	2eme	45	echec	2017-2018	
e002	el02	2eme	3eme	60	reussite	2018-2019	

Figure 26: Ranking list interface

B. PRESENTATION OF SOURCE CODES

```php
if(isset($_POST["enr_el"])){

    $code_ec2=$_POST["code_ec2"];
    $matel=$_POST["matel"];
    $nomel=$_POST["nomel"];
    $post=$_POST["post"];
    $prenom=$_POST["prenom"];$genre=$_POST["genre"];
    $daten=$_POST["daten"];
    $lieun=$_POST["lieun"];
    $adel=$_POST["adel"];$nationalite=$_POST["nationalite"];
    $req=$bdd->query("insert into eleve(code_ec,mat_el,nom,post,prenom,genre,daten,lieun,adresse_el,nationalite)values('$code_ec2','$matel',
    if($req){
        header("location:../adm/index_ex.php?msg=ok");
    }
    else{

        header("location:../adm/index_ex.php?msg=erreur");}
}
```

Figure 27: student registration code

```php
if(isset($_POST["enr_dem"])){
    $code_ec=$_POST["code_ec"];
    $matel=$_POST["matel"];
    $ec_dest=$_POST["ec_dest"];
    $motif=$_POST["motif"];
    $req=$bdd->query("insert into demande(code_ec,mat_el,ecole_dest,motif,etat,date_dmd)values('$code_ec','$matel','$ec_dest','$motif','n
if($req){
    header("location:../adm/index_eco.php?msg=ok");
}
else{

    header("location:../adm/index_eco.php?msg=erreur");}
}
```

Figure 28: Registration code for a student transfer request

GENERAL CONCLUSION

In short, our work focused on the development of an application to facilitate the monitoring of pupils' schooling within the Likasi sub-division inspectorate.

I.   We have presented the various stages leading up to the implementation of this palliative solution.

We began by identifying the difficulties encountered by the sub-division, mainly in SERNIE, with a view to finding an appropriate solution.

Our investigations revealed that considerable time was wasted in certain operations, such as searching for a document that was a long time in the past, and that difficulties were encountered in listing schools and pupils, as well as school vagrancy in different schools.

As a response to these various problems, we proposed the computerization of the service responsible for managing the school curriculum of students enrolled in primary, secondary and technical education in the urban city of Likasi.

In order to carry out our research, interview, documentary and direct observation techniques were of paramount importance. What's more, the UML modeling language and the UP unified process were used to support the needs analysis and design of our web application via the various UML diagrams covering the functional, dynamic and static aspects of development.

However, there is still room for improvement, such as enhancing the application with certain functionalities.

BIBLIOGRAPHY

A. Work

✓ KAZADI KIMBU and KALUNGA MAWAZO, *Les méthodes de recherche et d'analyse en sciences sociales et humaines*, EDUPC/Lubumbashi, 2013

✓ RONGERE and MULUMBATI NG, *manuel sociologie général*, Ed. Africa, Lubumbashi 1980

✓ Ibrahima Lo, *Les méthodes de recherche scientifique en sciences sociales,* ed. Alto Aubier, Paris, 1995

✓ Jean-Louis Loubet del Bayle, Initiation aux méthodes des sciences sociales(2000), Toulouse

✓ J.Batiste , *Merise, Guide pratique : modélisation des données et des traitements,* new edition, ENI, Paris,

✓ F.DIGALLO, Methodologie des systemes d'informations-merise,CNAM ANGOULEME, 2001-2002, Paris

✓ J.Batiste , *Merise, Guide pratique : modélisation des données et des traitements,* new edition, ENI, Paris,

✓ _ P. Roques, *les cahiers du programmeur UML2, Modéliser une application web*, ed. Eyrolles,4e dition, 2008,

✓ P. Roques, *les cahiers du programmeur UML2, Modéliser une application web, Eyrolles, 4th edition, 2008*

✓ P. Roque and F. Vallée, *UML2 in action, from needs analysis to design,* 4th ed, EYROLLES, Paris

✓ L. Welling and L. Thomson, *PHP & MYSQL,* Pearson, 4th Ed

B. Websites

✓ http:// En.m.Wikipedia.org

✓ http://web.mysql.com/why-mysql/benchmark.html

✓ Http:// www.larousse.fr

✓ *https://cordial.fr*

✓ *http://definition-simple.com*

✓ http ://developpez.com

More
Books!

info@omniscriptum.com
www.omniscriptum.com
OMNIScriptum

Printed by Books on Demand GmbH, Norderstedt / Germany